COURAGE

Arnold Schwarzenegger congratulates some winners at the Special Olympics.

THE VALUES LIBRARY

COURAGE

Ellen Kahaner

THE ROSEN PUBLISHING GROUP, INC.

NEW YORK

Published in 1990 by The Rosen Publishing Group, Inc.
29 East 21st Street, New York, NY 10010.

First Edition
Copyright 1990 by The Rosen Publishing Group, Inc.

Printed in Canada
Bound in the United States of America

Library of Congress Cataloging-in-Publication Data

Kahaner, Ellen.
    Courage / Ellen Kahaner.
    (The Values library)
    Includes bibliographical references.
    Index.
    Summary: Defines courage and discusses its importance in life.
    ISBN 0-8239-1112-8
    1. Courage—Juvenile literature. [1. Courage.   2. Conduct of
life.] I. Title. II. Series.
BJ1533.C8K34   1990
179'.6—dc20

89-48774
CIP
AC

C O N T E N T S

By protesting segregation in the 1960s, many blacks risked brutal treatment.

WHAT IS COURAGE?

ON DECEMBER 1, 1955, ROSA PARKS MADE HISTORY. Rosa
Parks was 43 years old and black. The law at that time
said blacks had to sit at the back of the bus. Even though
75 percent of the riders were black, the law in Montgomery, Alabama, said that blacks had to give their seats to
whites. Blacks had to enter the bus from the back door if
the bus was crowded. Whites sat in the front. Blacks sat
in the back. Segregation was law.

Rosa Parks was a secretary of the Montgomery chapter
of the NAACP (National Association for the Advancement
of Colored People). The NAACP was fighting the laws
that made blacks second-class citizens and denied them
equal opportunities. Rosa Parks decided to defy the law.
The NAACP told her to go ahead.

On December 1, 1955, Rosa Parks got on a bus heading
up Cleveland Avenue. She sat down in the first row of
the middle section of seats. She had worked all day, and
she was tired. The bus was crowded. One white man
was left standing. The bus driver ordered Rosa Parks to
give her seat to the white man. She refused.

The white passengers looked at Rosa Parks in disbelief. How dare she refuse? No black person had ever refused before.

"Well, I'm going to call the police and have you arrested," the driver said.

"You may do that," said Rosa Parks.

She knew that she was defying a whole system. The system said that black people were not as good as white people. She knew her saying "no" was an act of defiance. That simple "no" took tremendous courage.

The police came and took Rosa Parks to jail. But the news of her defiant action spread like wildfire. It inspired other blacks to action. It made them aware of something. They realized that they, too, could refuse to ride in the back of the bus.

The black leaders of Montgomery called for a bus boycott. A boycott is the act of joining together in refusing to buy, sell or deal with an organization to punish it. They asked other blacks to support Rosa Parks by refusing to ride the bus. Rosa Parks was in jail, but she was not alone.

More and more blacks joined the boycott. They chose to walk long distances to work. They were not stopped by the insults from whites along the streets. They were not afraid of their employers' disapproval.

Rosa Parks' action and the boycott resulted in a lawsuit that went all the way to the United States Supreme Court.

Rosa Parks courageously
defied a system that
treated blacks unfairly.

The Supreme Court ruled in favor of the boycotters. The
public bus system throughout the United States had to be
integrated. The new law permitted seating on any public
bus on a "first come, first served" basis. Whites could no
longer treat blacks as inferior human beings without vio-
lating the law.

One black woman and the black people who joined her in the boycott changed the law. One woman's courage changed history.

You may not change the history of a country every time you stand up for what you believe is right. But you can change what happens in your life and in the lives of the people around you.

Here are examples of situations where *you* may choose to act courageously.

• Everyone in your class is excluding the new kid and making fun of him. Do you stand up for him?

• You go to a party where the coolest kids from school are doing drugs. Do you leave? Do you speak out?

• Your history teacher makes a statement in class that you believe is wrong. Do you say something?

• You spend many hours trying to understand the math homework, but you still don't get it. Do you seek help?

• You have an argument with your best friend. Later you find out that you've made a big mistake. Do you apologize?

• All the kids on your block are teasing one kid who is "different." Do you join them? Or do you stand up for the kid even though it may make you unpopular?

Courage comes from the Latin word *cor*, which means heart. Today, courage can mean doing what you believe in your heart.

Admitting you need help
from a tutor can be an
act of courage.

Chapter One

In a moment of courage, the feeling of "I can" overpow-
ers "I can't." You are not sure what will happen. You hold
your breath. You try.

Imagine yourself doing one of these things.

•You say to everyone in your class, "Leave him alone!
How would you feel if everyone was picking on you? Cut
it out!"

•You say to the host of the party, "I'm leaving. Doing
drugs is stupid."

•You say to your history teacher, "Excuse me. My
uncle was in Vietnam and that isn't the way he talked
about the war."

•You say to your math teacher, "I need help. I'd like to
sign up for math tutoring."

•You call your best friend. "Hi. It's me. Look, I'm
sorry I picked a fight with you. The main thing is, I acted
like a jerk. Can we still be friends?"

•You defend the kid under attack. "Hey, that's really
mean. Who are you to talk about someone like that." And
you say to the kid, "Come on, let's go home together."

When you take a stand, you don't know how it will end.
Your classmates could turn against you. Your teacher
could get mad. The math tutor may not have time to help
you. She may confuse you even more. Your friend might
hang up on you. The other kids might make fun of you.

Courage involves risk. You won't always know how something is going to turn out. But at least you have tried. You have taken a stand for something you believe in. And that is what courage is all about.

When is it important to be courageous? How has courageous action affected our past? How does it affect our present? How will it affect our future? This book will answer these questions. You will see men and women who are models of courage. But this book also shows how to be courageous in your own life. You will see how you can change your day-to-day life.

2

WHERE COURAGE IS NECESSARY

WHEN IS COURAGE NECESSARY? Imagine what might happen
if you are not courageous. Thinking may help you to act.
What if Rosa Parks had gone to the back of the bus?

This chapter is about people who chose to act with
courage. The stories are examples of physical, emotional
and spiritual courage. They are about politics, business
and education.

Courage In Politics

In 1987, Governor Madeleine M. Kunin of Vermont
spoke at the Women's Political Caucus in Portland, Ore-
gon. The subject was "political courage." Political courage
is the courage to take action for what you believe is right.

"Political courage stems from a number of sources—
anger, pain, love, hate. Anger at a world which rushes
towards menacing displays of power. Pain at a world
which ignores the suffering of its homeless, its elderly, its
children. Hatred toward the injustice which occurs daily as
the strong overpower the weak. And love for the dream
of peace on earth. First you have to want to change the

Governor Madeline Kunin of Vermont explained that political courage is doing what you believe is right.

world, then you find a way to do it," Governor Kunin said.

Governor Kunin spoke about why it was important, even urgent for her to be in politics. It gave her the chance to turn her values into public action to affect people's lives for the better: improving the schools, protecting the environment, supporting nuclear disarmament.

In 1988, Governor Kunin led a delegation from Vermont

to the Soviet Union. She wanted to set up a sister-state relationship with the Soviet state of Karelia. A sister-state relationship means two states from different countries "adopt"
each other. Their people exchange visits, art, music, ideas,
and experiences.

It takes political courage to make a better world.

Courage In Business

Roger Boisjoly (boys-jolly) was a top engineer at Morton
Thiokol, Inc., a Utah-based firm. Thiokol was the company
that manufactured the solid rocket booster for the space
shuttle *Challenger.*

In 1985, Boisjoly noticed that the company was using
faulty O-rings in manufacturing the rocket's booster. O-
rings are rubber seals that are placed between the rocket's
joints. These seals could fail in cold weather. Before the
Challenger launch, Boisjoly and other co-workers warned
their bosses at Thiokol and top managers at NASA (National
Aeronautics and Space Administration) about the faulty O-
rings. Boisjoly was afraid the O-rings could seriously
threaten the *Challenger* flight.

The bosses ignored the warning and proceeded with the
schedule. On January 18, 1986, The *Challenger* was
launched into space as planned, and exploded seven sec-
onds later. The entire crew was killed. Sometimes speaking

Roger Boisjoly lost his job.
He had the courage to
warn people about a
defective part on the
space shuttle *Challenger.*

up does not change things. But Roger Boisjoly tried.

What happened to Roger Boisjoly? Thiokol moved him to a less important job. Soon after, he took a long sick leave from the company.

Roger Boisjoly spoke out and risked his career. Does he regret it? "I couldn't live with any self respect if I didn't speak up," he said. It takes courage to speak up at work. And it is even harder to do if what you say goes against what people want to believe. Boisjoly knows he tried to save the people who perished in the *Challenger*. It does not matter what his bosses at Thiokol did with the information he gave them.

Although your situation may be different from Roger Boisjoly's, the important issue is the same; whether you are asking for a raise, complaining about working conditions or challenging how you are treated. If you do not *speak up* and *try*, it will become easier to accept wrongdoing. It will be easier to let the next wrong go by, and the next.

Courage In School

In May 1983, Robert R. Reynolds, the principal of Hazelwood East High School near St. Louis, Missouri, decided to censor two articles from the student newspaper, *The Spectrum*. Censoring means denying the right of information to people because the censor thinks it is not proper or fit for

The *Challenger* explosion happened in spite of one man's warnings.

The Supreme Court ruled
against a student news-
paper's demands for
freedom of the press.

those people. One article that was censored was about
teenage pregnancy. The other was about the children of
divorce.

The Spectrum staff was outraged. What gave the principal the right to violate their First Amendment rights, which
are guaranteed in the Constitution? The First Amendment
guarantees that government officials, including public

school officials, cannot violate the right to free expression.

The student journalists went to the American Civil Liberties Union and asked for help. Leslie D. Edwards, the lawyer who took their case, filed a suit against the Hazelwood East School District Board. This case went all the way to the Supreme Court, the highest court in the United States.

The Supreme Court voted 5-3 against the students. Schools have the right to censor student speech if it is an activity sponsored and given money by the school. The school newspaper, the justices decided, is not a "public forum." This means that the newspaper is not an outlet for student expression. Justice Byron R. White, for the majority, said that "no violation of First Amendment rights had occurred."

One Supreme Court judge who strongly disagreed with this decision, Justice William J. Brennan, called the majority rule, "brutal censorship" and "thought control." Justice Brennan also said that this action would teach students "not to respect the diversity of ideas that is fundamental to the American system."

It took courage for Justice William J. Brennan to speak out against the decision. It took great courage for the East Hazelwood students to fight censorship. Although they didn't win the case, there are still ways to protect the students. Since the Hazelwood decision, some states—including

Justice William J. Brennan disagreed with the majority of the Supreme Court when he supported a school newspaper's right to free speech.

Illinois, Massachusetts, New Jersey, Rhode Island, Wisconsin and Wyoming—have moved to pass laws to prevent school officials from censoring student publications. The Student Press Law Center in Washington, D.C., is leading the campaign to watch the way the Supreme Court ruling will be applied. It is offering assistance to students to fight censorship.

Sometimes, courage is necessary in daily life. We often have to confront a problem at home or at school. This can be seen in the following story.

Marcie was getting ready for school one morning. She found her father asleep on the couch in his clothes. A half-filled wine glass was balanced on his chest. She tried to wake him up, but he wouldn't move. She ran to her parent's bedroom and woke up her mother. "What's wrong with Daddy?" she wanted to know. Her mother told her that father had been fired from his job because of his drinking. He was very upset.

It takes courage to confront family problems such as alcoholism.

The next night Marcie heard her parents fighting. The door to their bedroom was closed, so Marcie could only hear some of what they said.

"I feel useless as a weed," she heard her father say. A little later, Marcie heard the front door slam. She ran to the bedroom. Her mother was crying.

"What's going on?" Marcie asked. Her mother told Marcie that she had tried to talk to her father about a very serious problem, his drinking. Her father was an alcoholic. Alcoholics are people who are unable to control their drinking. Drinking causes major problems in their lives.

Marcie felt her stomach drop to the floor. She had heard the word many times, but never about someone she knew personally. "Why would Daddy do this to himself, to us?" she asked her mother. "Doesn't he love us?" Marcie felt scared. "What does this mean? Is the family falling apart? What did Daddy say?"

"He says he doesn't have a problem," her mother said with a worried look. "I told him that the only way he was going to get better was by admitting that he has a problem. Then he must ask for help. He needs treatment. A person can die from alcoholism."

Marcie was very upset. "What if Daddy doesn't stop drinking? Will he end up a bum on the streets? Will he die?"

Support from an organization like Alateen can give a person courage to deal with an alcoholic parent.

"First of all," Marcie's mother told her, "most alcoholics are not bums. They are men or women with families, jobs, and responsibilities, like your father."

"It's my fault, isn't it?" Marcie said.

"It is not your fault," her mother said firmly. "But it is common to feel that way. We need help too," her mother said, "so we don't go crazy with this." She went through some papers and handed Marcie a pamphlet. It said "Alateen" on the cover, and underneath, "for people from 12-21 years of age who have a family member or friend with a drinking problem." Marcie stared at the pamphlet. "How is Alateen going to help?" she asked.

"Alateen is a self-help group," her mother said. A self-help group is a group of people who meet and help each other. It is free of charge, and there are no professional counselors. People with the same problem are all there to give each other support. These groups are very successful in helping people to help themselves.

"I'm going to join Al-anon, which is a group for adults," her mother said.

"How did you find these?" Marcie asked.

"In the phone book, under 'alcoholism.'" Her mother smiled. "It is not hard to find help. The hard part is deciding that you need it."

"I guess it takes courage to admit you have a problem

and get help," Marcie said.

"We're going to need a lot of courage," her mother agreed, "and a lot of help."

Physical Courage

"At first I thought it would be impossible to choreograph (to design dance movements) from a wheelchair," said Barry Martin, founder and director of the Deja Vu Dance Theater. "All things are possible if you believe."

Barry Martin is a native New Yorker. He studied dance at the Alvin Ailey American Dance Center as a scholarship student. He graduated from college with honors and began a promising career as a dancer.

In 1983 a tragic event drastically changed Barry Martin's life. During a dance tour, he was in a terrible automobile accident. He was left a quadriplegic (qua-dra-plee-gic). This meant that Barry Martin lost all ability to move his arms and legs.

Although Barry Martin could not dance, his vision of how he wanted people to move, his vision of dance, remained bright.

Here is a man who could have given up. Certainly everyone expected Barry Martin to end his career as a choreographer. Choreographers almost always demonstrate dance movements themselves. They show the

Even though he is not able to dance, Barry Martin returned to his career as a choreographer.

motion they are imagining to the dancer. Barry Martin couldn't do that.

After a year of treatment, he decided he would return to his career as a choreographer. He founded the Deja Vu Dance Theater.

The dancers in the company learn their movements completely through talking with Martin. "They interpret my ideas," Martin said.

Spiritual Courage

Albert Schweitzer is one of the first people we think of when we look for examples of spiritual courage. Dr. Schweitzer was a brilliant man. He would have been successful at anything he decided to do.

Born in 1875 in Alsace, Schweitzer was educated in Germany and France. During his life he was a philosopher, a clergyman, a missionary, a writer on religious subjects and a physician. Schweitzer was a talented musician. He was skilled at playing the organ. He was famous for his versions of the works of J.S. Bach, one of the world's greatest composers. And he was an authority on Bach's life and works. He was also a gifted organ builder. Any one of those careers would have been a full life for an ordinary man.

Schweitzer decided to spend his time until the age of 30

in science, music and preaching. Then he would spend
the rest of his life making things better for mankind.

In 1902, Albert Schweitzer decided to become a medical
missionary. He studied medicine, and then raised money
to build a hospital. He gave concerts for the Paris Bach
Society. He also received money from the worshippers he
served as a minister. He built his hospital in Lambarene, in
French Equatorial Africa, which is now called Gabon. The
hospital opened in 1913. Before then, thousands of Afri-
can families had no medical care at all. He continued to
receive contributions for his good works. His hospital
grew and grew.

Dr. Schweitzer received the Nobel Peace Prize in 1952.
He used the prize money to improve his hospital. He also
set up a special treatment unit for sufferers with leprosy.
Leprosy is a disease that attacks and destroys parts of the
body. Lepers were treated very badly and made to stay
apart from other people. Dr. Schweitzer devoted part of
his work to easing their physical suffering and their personal hardships.

Dr. Schweitzer could have spent his life in luxury, richly
rewarded for using his many talents. Instead, he lived
among the less fortunate, making their lives more bearable.
And in all the years in Africa he never stopped studying
and writing. His writings were about philosophy and

Albert Schweitzer devoted much of his life to helping sick people in Africa.

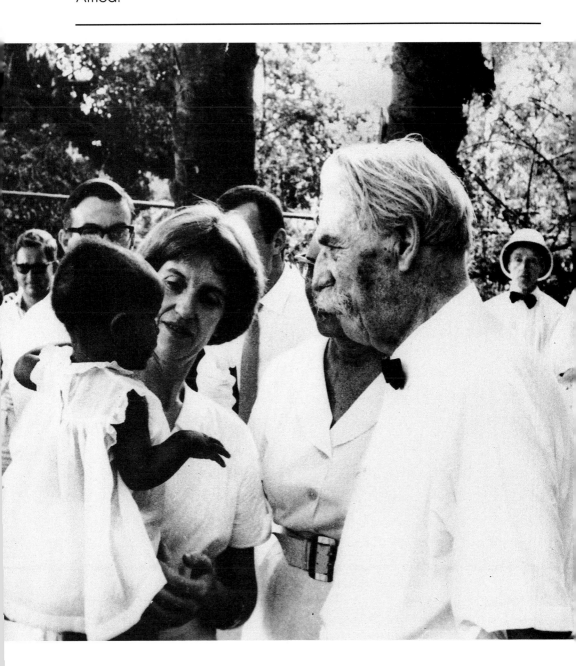

Desmond Tutu is working to end racial segregation in South Africa.
This is an example of spiritual courage.

religion. He also wrote about his life and work in Africa.

During his lifetime the world changed a great deal. Dr. Schweitzer continued to care about what happened to everyone. He never gave up his work in Lambarene. But he traveled and spoke all over the world about things that were important to him.

In 1957, Dr. Albert Schweitzer took on another important job. He spoke out against nuclear weapons. The nations of the world were in a race to build and test atomic bombs. Dr. Schweitzer was afraid of radioactive fallout from these bombs. He knew that it was dangerous to humans and to all forms of life.

Until his death in 1965, Dr. Albert Schweitzer spent every day serving his fellow man with every thought and action. He made the world a better place. His life has been an inspiration to others as well. Before Dr. Martin Luther King, Jr., or Mother Teresa, or Bishop Desmond Tutu, Dr. Schweitzer taught us the meaning of spiritual courage.

3

PEOPLE FAMOUS FOR THEIR COURAGE

MOST OF US DO NOT FEEL VERY COURAGEOUS. One way to learn to be courageous is by studying people famous for their courage. These people are known as role models. A role model is someone whose behavior sets an example you can learn from.

In this chapter you will see people famous for their courage in history, in war, in science and in literature. They can teach you how to be courageous in your own life.

In History: **Thoreau, Gandhi, King**

The writings of Henry David Thoreau are famous throughout the world. His name is as well-known today as it was in the mid-nineteenth century. In 1846, Thoreau lived and worked in Concord, Massachusetts.

Thoreau loved this country very much. But he believed that some of the events of his time would have serious effects on the nation's future.

Thoreau was an abolitionist (a-bo-li-shun-ist). That means he believed that slavery should be declared against

Henry David Thoreau had strong beliefs about American policy. He went to jail for upholding them.

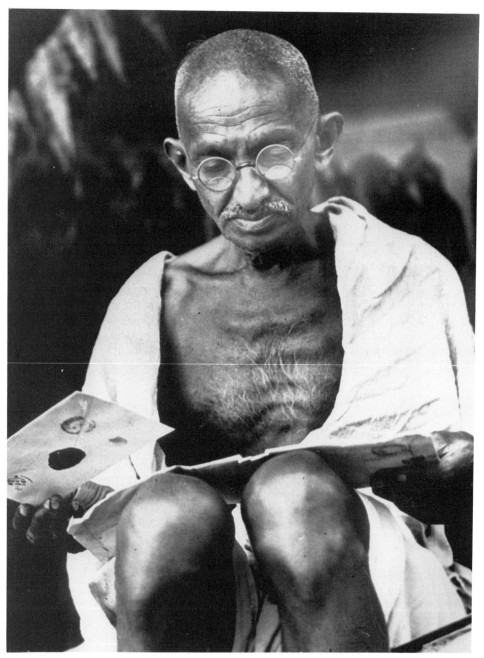

"Mahatma" Gandhi carried on the idea of nonviolent civil disobedience.

the law. At that time, the people of this country were divided in their opinions about slavery. Many believed as Thoreau did, especially in the North. But many Americans, especially in the South, believed that slavery was necessary for the success of American cotton and tobacco farmers.

Thoreau was also against the Mexican War, which began in 1846. Texas had won its independence from Mexico, and joined the United States in 1845. There was a disagreement about the location of the border between Mexico and Texas. President James Polk sent troops under General Zachary Taylor to fight the Mexican army.

Thoreau wanted to express his disapproval of these actions.

Thoreau decided the best way to oppose slavery and the Mexican War was to refuse to pay taxes. He was saying to his government, "I will not pay for things I think are wrong." He would not support the war with his tax money.

He was arrested and put in jail because he failed to pay his taxes. His friends and neighbors got together and paid the tax money. They did not tell Thoreau what they had done. He was told he had to leave the jail, because his taxes had been paid.

Thoreau was very unhappy about being released. He explained his position in a public speech to his fellow townsmen. If every citizen who hated slavery would join him in jail, the government would be forced to choose

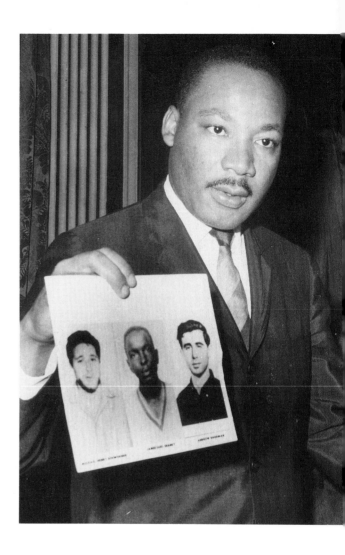

Dr. Martin Luther King, Jr. used civil disobedience to change unfair laws in the American South. *(From left to right),* 1.King holds a picture of three civil rights workers that were killed in Mississippi; 2. giving his famous "I have a dream" speech in Washington D.C.; 3.accepting the Nobel Prize for peace.

between having its best citizens in jail or having to put an end to slavery. The idea Thoreau was suggesting is called civil disobedience.

According to *A Topical Dictionary of American Government and Politics,* civil disobedience is an action taken by a person or a group. They publicly, nonviolently and with no resistance to arrest, break a law in order to bring about a change in the law or social structure.

"There is no doubt that Thoreau's ideas greatly influenced my movement in India," Mahatma Gandhi said to an

American journalist. Gandhi led a successful movement in the 1930s and 1940s to free India from British rule. He led the people in *nonviolent* civil disobedience.

The Reverend Dr. Martin Luther King, Jr., visited India in 1959. He discussed Gandhi's philosophy of nonviolent resistance with people who had known him. Soon after, King used direct-action nonviolent tactics inspired by the teachings of Gandhi (sit-ins, protest marches, bus boycotts). They were valuable weapons in the fight against racial segregation in the deep South in the early 1960s.

Chapter Three

King was arrested at a protest to end segregation at lunch counters and discrimination in hiring practices. In a letter he wrote from a Birmingham, Alabama jail, King spelled out his philosophy of nonviolence:

You may well ask: 'Why direct action? Why sit-ins, marches and so forth? Isn't negotiation a better path?' You are quite right in calling for negotiation. Indeed, this is the very purpose of direct action. Nonviolent direct action seeks to create such a crisis and foster such a tension that a community which has constantly refused to negotiate is forced to confront the issue. It seeks so to dramatize the issue that it can no longer be ignored. . . . We know through painful experience that freedom is never voluntarily given by the oppressor; it must be demanded by the oppressed.

In 1964, the American Civil Rights Act was passed. This law said the federal government would protect the rights of all citizens to be treated equally under the law. It outlawed making people use separate drinking fountains and lunch counters because of the color of their skin. It said that all people who were qualified should have equal opportunity for jobs.

In the late 1960s and the 1970s, anti-Vietnam war protesters successfully used demonstrations and sit-ins to protest American involvement in Vietnam. This opposition led President Lyndon Johnson to decide not to run for a sec-

ond term of office. Eventually they also forced President
Richard Nixon to end the Vietnam War.

Today, thousands of protesters are arrested in the
United States each year for acts of civil disobedience
against nuclear weapons plants and nuclear power plants.
Protesters have occupied the construction site at the
Seabrook Nuclear Power Plant in New Hampshire. They
blocked the huge Diablo Canyon Nuclear Power Plant
under construction in California. They blocked the en-
trances to California's Lawrence Livermore Laboratory,
which designs nuclear weapons. Over one million dem-
onstrators marched in the streets of New York City on
June 12, 1982, in the biggest peace rally in American history, to stop the arms race.

In War: **Muriel Gardiner**

Muriel Gardiner was a well respected doctor who studied in Vienna before World War II. She was also a rich
American, who made it possible for hundreds of people to
escape the Nazis in the 1930s.

Dr. Gardiner knew that her actions placed her in as
much danger as the people she was helping to escape.
But doing the right thing was more important to her than
staying out of danger.

Later, Muriel Gardiner was asked if she was aware,
back in 1934, that she was doing anything extraordinary.

In the movie *Julia*, Vanessa Redgrave played a character based on Muriel Gardiner.

She replied, "I was afraid. But extraordinary? No, I don't believe I was aware of that. It simply needed to be done."

The ability to do what is needed to be done in war has nothing to do with fancy promises and slogans or flashy uniforms. It has to do with making a commitment to life, to living.

In Science: Galileo Galilei

Sometimes an idea is so frightening to people that they try to destroy it. They make it a crime for people to believe in it. The idea that the earth moves around the sun was once considered not only revolutionary, but criminal. An Italian mathematician, astronomer, and physicist named Galileo Galilei wrote a book agreeing with this idea. He was considered a criminal in the eyes of the Roman Catholic Church. The church insisted that the earth was the center of the universe. Everyone thought that all the planets revolved around the earth. Galileo, a keen observer of natural events, disagreed. Based on what he saw through a telescope, he believed the planets revolved around the sun. The church was outraged. Galileo's views went against what the church wanted people to believe.

In 1616, the church issued a decree. Galileo had to promise never to talk about his ideas again. Galileo agreed. Seven years later, a friend of Galileo's became the Pope. The Pope is the head of the Catholic Church. Galileo was allowed to publish a book, *Dialogue Concerning the Two Chief World Systems*. The book supported Galileo's earlier views. He could no longer keep them to himself. They were too important. This book was hailed as a masterpiece throughout Europe.

The Pope turned against Galileo because he had broken his promise to the church. Church officials put Galileo under house arrest for life. This meant Galileo could never travel away from home. He also had to publicly deny his views again. Galileo agreed, so that his life would be spared. But his work had challenged how everyone saw the world.

Galileo had the courage to publish his beliefs even though it put his life in danger.

Throughout his life, Galileo remained a loyal Catholic. But he believed that science and religion must be kept separate.

Before his death in 1642, Galileo had the manuscript of his second book smuggled out of Italy. It was taken to a publisher in Holland. The publication of this book, *Two New Sciences*, marks the beginning of modern physics.

In Literature: **Why the Caged Bird Sings**

Acting with courage is easier if you don't feel alone. It is easier if you know what another person's life is like. But how can you know how it felt to live fifty years ago in a place you've never seen? What it's like to be a person of another race or religion? Another sex? One way to share another person's experiences is by reading. Literature helps you to feel less lonely and more like other people.

I Know Why the Caged Bird Sings is Maya Angelou's story of her own life. It takes place in her home town of Stamps, Arkansas. The year is 1940. The main character is Marguerite Johnson. Marguerite Johnson is black and at-tends Lafayette Country Training School, a segregated school.

Segregation means to separate by race. A segregated school is one that is all white or all black. In the South, segregated schools for blacks were poorly staffed and maintained, with few resources for learning.

A famous chapter of the book, "Graduation," has been reprinted in many high school and college readers. Marguerite Johnson is about to graduate as one of the top students in her eighth grade class. Not only is graduation an important event in her life, it is a major event for the entire community. Everyone looks forward to graduation with excitement and hope for a better future.

Finally, the great day arrives. But Marguerite Johnson has a strong sense that something is going to go wrong. As she and her family walk to the graduation ceremony, the windows of the school look cold and unfriendly. The graduates march into the auditorium and take their seats on the stage. The principal leads them in singing the national anthem and the pledge of allegiance. Then he surprisingly skips the singing of the Negro National Anthem, a song of pride. The class always sings the anthem at assemblies.

Then the principal introduces an unexpected speaker. Marguerite notices his voice changes from the strong voice she has always enjoyed to something weak. The speaker is a white man from the school district named Edward Donleavy.

Mr. Donleavy announces the exciting improvements that are due at the white high school. A real artist is coming to teach art. They will have new microscopes and chemistry equipment in their laboratories. He announces no such improvements for Lafayette County Training School. Finally he has something to say about Lafayette. One of Fisk University's best basketball players came from Lafayette Country Training School. Marguerite gets this message from his speech:

"The white kids were going to have a chance to become Galileos and Madame Curies and Edisons and Gauguins. Our boys (the girls weren't even in on it) would try to be Jesse Owenses and Joe Louises."

Marguerite is furious. What gives this man the right to decide who her heroes should be? To Marguerite, graduation is finished before her name is even called. It is an awful feeling. She feels she has no control over her life. It seems her future has already been decided.

Suddenly, there is a hush in the auditorium. Henry Reed, the conservative straight-A student, puts his prepared remarks aside. He turns his back to the audience and addresses his fellow graduates. He begins to speak the words of the Negro national anthem. The students start to sing along. Then the parents in the audience stand up and sing. The younger brothers and sisters join in.

Marguerite hears the words as if for the first time. She is greatly moved by the sense of history, struggle and solidarity in the words. When the song is over, Henry Reed bows his head and says "thank you." Marguerite, who

Maya Angelou's book still inspires many young black women.

moments earlier felt furious and despairing, now feels tremendous pride.

"I was no longer simply a member of the proud graduating class of 1940, I was a proud member of this wonderful, beautiful Negro race."

Breaking a mood of despair requires courage. For Henry Reed, Marguerite Johnson and the other students of the class of 1940 to stand up together and raise their voices took great courage, and great pride.

Characters in literature who take a stand can inspire us by their example. We can become more aware of injustices around us. We can understand how to act to help make a better world.

4

WHY COURAGE IS ADMIRED

WHO DO YOU ADMIRE? According to Tom W. Smith, of the National Opinion Research Center at the University of Chicago, most people admire people "dedicated to serving the common good." The common good is something that benefits everyone: a cleaner environment, world peace, a cure for disease, better schools.

One reason courage is admired is because a courageous person does what is right, in spite of the "what ifs" of life:
- What if your parents disagree with you?
- What if your teacher gets mad?
- What if someone stronger comes along?
- What if your friends laugh at you?

Another reason people admire courage is because acting courageously makes you feel good. It is a way of respecting yourself. When you see an act of courage, you may want to act that way too. If you see someone standing up for the new kid at school, you could stand up with them. Another person's courage gives you the idea, and sometimes the opportunity, to be courageous too.

Acts of courage can change things. Here are some ideas to keep in mind.

• Remember what courage is and what courage is not. Courage usually means taking a chance by standing up for something you believe. Courage is not taking a foolish risk. It is not courageous to be a daredevil. These kinds of actions do nothing for the "common good." And they probably have very little to do with what you believe in.

• If possible, talk to other people who support your actions before going ahead. This will help you feel less alone, particularly if you are taking an unpopular stand.

• Be aware that you won't always be greeted with open arms and a big hug for acting with courage. In the story in chapter two, Marcie's father may get very mad at her for taking a stand against his drinking. It may get so bad at home that she has to move out of the house. These are very painful things, but the truth is her father is endangering his life. She's acting to help him. But it doesn't mean that she might not feel emotional pain.

Keep in mind that courage can really help:

• Courage can make people aware of a problem. For example, Roger Boisjoly made the country aware of the dangers of corporations covering up their mistakes.

• Courage can lead to a better understanding between people. Governor Kunin visited the Soviet Union to set up a sister-state relationship. She encouraged the people who live in both countries to find out about each other and discuss how to solve problems.

•Courage raises questions that need to be asked. In a democracy, censorship goes against the Constitution. But because the people who questioned censorship were high school students, they were treated as if they were too young to decide. What do you think? Should eleventh graders have the right to decide what they can read? Courageous acts raise questions that need to be asked.

•Courage can affect the course of history, the present and the future. Rosa Parks' courageous action on the bus in Montgomery changed the course of history.

Acting courageously has a tremendous effect on you. By practicing courage you get better at it. It gets a bit easier. If you act courageously about one thing—even something like getting up on the dance floor and actually dancing—it might give you the courage to try something else, to try something harder. By acting courageously, you get more satisfaction from your own life. You'll get more out of living, whether you are:

- asking for a raise at your after-school job
- trying out for a part in the school play
- making a new friend
- meeting people different from yourself.

Courageous acts today pave the way for a safer future and a better world.

5

WHAT DOES IT TAKE TO BE COURAGEOUS?

WHAT DOES IT TAKE TO BE COURAGEOUS? Here are some things to consider about acting with courage. These are real suggestions for times when physical, emotional or spiritual courage is called for.

General Suggestions

•Think about whether you are taking a considered risk or taking a chance. Taking a considered risk means giving careful thought to the dangers involved in an action. Taking a chance is like gambling. You have very little if any control over what happens.

•If possible, get information about the risk you want to take. Learn how others have handled the same situation. Get instructions from a teacher or leader you can trust.

•Try to think of yourself as a role model for others—a younger brother or sister, your friends.

•Keep your personal "cheering squad" in mind; your friends and loved ones. It helps to know you are not alone and that other people support you.

•Timing is important. Sometimes waiting for the right

moment can make the difference. For example, if you want to break the news to your parents that you have decided to go away to college, don't blurt it out as they walk in the door from a hard day's work.

•Sometimes, in an emergency, there is no time to plan how to act. You have to trust what your heart tells you is right. Making a quick decision to help someone is an act of courage.

Physical Courage

There are many types of physical courage. Saving the life of a child by entering a burning building requires physical courage. Blind students learning how to swim need physical courage. If you are afraid to dance in front of people, getting up and boogie-ing at a party is courageous.

Depending on what type of physical action you take, some of the following suggestions may help:

•Think of specific actions that will help you overcome your fear. For example, if you are afraid of heights and you are looking out the window of a tall building, look at the horizon rather than straight down.

•According to Dr. Martin Symonds of the New York City Police Department, "acts of physical courage generally stem from a sense of relatedness to someone you

Rescuing people during an emergency takes physical courage.

love or to the general population." Keep people in mind. Acting with courage is hardest when you are alone.

•Sometimes people, especially girls, are taught to be afraid of getting hurt. They think of themselves as easily hurt. They are taught to be careful and not to play rough. This makes it very hard to take on a physical challenge. If you fall into this category, remember that you can learn how *not* to be afraid. You can become very strong. Try to find a step-by-step approach to learning a physical skill you want to have. It may feel frightening at first, but you'll find that your worst fears are just fears, not realities.

Emotional Courage

Acting with courage stirs up your emotions. Emotions are strong feelings that are often accompanied by physical changes. If you are feeling fearful, your heart might beat quickly, your palms sweat, and your voice shake. The reason there is an emotional side to courage is because it's not a "sure thing." You don't know how it will end.

Here are some suggestions for dealing with the emotional side of courage:

•Keep in mind that everyone gets scared. Very often what stops us from acting with courage is the fear that we are the only ones to feel this way; this scared, this terrified. Knowing that other people have felt the same way and have survived helps us feel that we will survive too.

•Courage is not the absence of fear. Being courageous is being able to act even if we have fear.

•Courage can be learned with practice. "Heroes evolve; they aren't born," said Dr. Ervin Staub of the University of Massachusetts. He was talking about the people who saved Jews from the concentration camps in Nazi Germany during World War II. "Once they had taken that step to hide someone for a day or two they began to see themselves differently, as someone who helps. What starts as mere willingness becomes intense involvement."

Spiritual Courage

Having the courage to act on values that are important to you takes spiritual courage. If you are having trouble finding the inner strength to stand up for what you believe in, consider these suggestions:

•Try to see your problems with a broader view. Remember the reasons for your actions and the value of acting with courage to yourself and those you love. Try to understand other people's acts of courage and the importance of their actions. Your personal difficulties may seem small compared to the bigger purpose you want to support.

•Decide whether the action you are taking is public or private. If it is a public action, such as protesting an injustice in your school, find other people and work together. You will be more successful working in a group than working alone. If the action is a private one, such as deciding to become a vegetarian, don't assume that what is right for you is right for everyone else. Make your own decisions, but remember they are *your* decisions. Don't get angry at people just because they don't share your own beliefs.

6

HOW COURAGE AFFECTS EVERYDAY LIFE

IT WAS JOHN'S FIRST DAY AT A NEW SCHOOL. He waited on the long cafeteria line to buy his lunch, but he didn't mind. In fact, he would have been happy to wait on line the entire period. He slid his tray along the metal rack, staring at the little bowls of mashed potatoes, red jello, orange covered "mystery" meat. He would rather stand in this line smelling the tomato soup and sour milk than face the large crowded room of strangers. Hundreds of new faces. There wasn't one single face that he had seen before.

His stomach was in a knot. He grabbed some food, hardly noticing what it was, and walked to the cashier. The knot in his stomach got tighter. He felt his palms start to sweat. He knew this feeling from his old school. It was fear. When he stood at the edge of the pool, motionless in the swimmer's ready crouch, before a swim team race, his heart would pound. His mouth would feel dry. "On your mark, get set..."

"One dollar and forty cents, please," the cashier said to him impatiently.

"Sorry," John said. He fumbled in his pocket for

change. Even his tray seemed to sweat as the dishes slid from one side to the other. He stood still and looked around. What if someone noticed his braces and called him metal mouth? Why hadn't he worn jeans like everyone else? What if he sat down and was told the seat was taken?

Wait a minute, John thought. No one was going to mash his face in for just sitting down. He saw a table with some empty seats and walked toward it. Hold on. He didn't want to sit alone for the rest of the year. He sucked in his breath and swallowed hard. Okay. Just do it. Just find some people that look friendly and sit somewhere. Anywhere. Move yourself. One foot in front of the other. You can't stand here like a statue. He saw a bunch of guys laughing and talking. He recognized one of them from Mr. Boyle's homeroom.

"Hi, mind if I sit here?" He heard his voice crack.

"It's all yours," one of them said.

"Actually we were saving that seat," the other one said.

"For who?" the guy from his homeroom said.

"Don Mattingly, but he's going to be a little late," they all laughed. "If he comes, you'll have to get up."

"I think I can handle that," John said, sliding into the seat. "My name is John."

"I'm Eric."

"Greg."

The others introduced themselves.

"What do you think of Boyle?" Eric asked him.

John took a deep breath and said, "Uh, not much." The other guys laughed.

"I hear he's a real turkey," Greg said and grinned. He had a mouth full of braces.

John watched out of the corners of his eyes. The guys were eating their lunches, looking up at the clock over the cashier's counter, nothing special. Their talk was easy— about new teachers, sports, movies. He felt a huge wave of relief. Maybe this year wouldn't be so bad after all.

When John realized that he didn't want to spend the year eating by himself, he took action. He wanted to make friends. He overcame his fear and he succeeded. That's courage.

Have you ever walked into a room full of strangers where you knew absolutely no one? Maybe it was at school. It could have been at camp, at work, or at a party. What can you do to help yourself? When you're courageous it's not just for the good of other people. There's something in it for you too! If John hadn't acted, he would have sat by himself in a corner and felt miserable. Without courage, you can't get what you need.

Courage breeds courage. This means that acting courageously leads to more courageous acts. It gets easier the second time and the third time around. That's how you develop the confidence to act the way you want to act. The same fears may come up. John may still feel afraid that the kids will reject him—but now he has had the experience of what it was like to get what he wanted. Even if the kids had rejected him— if they were having a private conversation and said, "no, you can't sit here"—he would still notice that he survived. He might have to find another table, but he would live to tell the tale. And he would leave knowing he made an effort. He tried to be a friend.

So how does courage affect your everyday life? The only way to have self-respect is to have the courage to be who you are. Who you are includes what you feel, what you think, what you want, and how you act. It takes courage to be honest about who you are.

Glossary: *Explaining New Words*

abolitionist Someone who believed that slavery was wrong and should be against the law.

alcoholic Someone who is unable to control his or her drinking.

boycott The act of joining together in refusing to buy, sell, or deal with an organization to punish it.

caucus To meet in a group in order to make decisions.

censor To deny the right of information to people on the grounds that it is not proper or fit for those people.

choreograph To design dance movements.

civil disobedience A peaceful act of protest that involves disobeying the law.

collaboration To make a combined effort; work together.

defiance The act of openly resisting something or going against someone.

extraordinary Special; not ordinary or average.

injustice Something that is wrong or unfair.

precariousness The state or quality of being unsteady or shaky.

quadriplegic A person who is completely paralyzed from the neck down.

role model Someone whose behavior sets an example you can learn from.

segregation Separation by race.

status quo The way things are.

sister-state A relationship between two states from different countries. They "adopt" each other and exchange art, music, ideas and experiences.

solidarity Common feeling among people in a group.

For Further Reading

Angelou, Maya. *I Know Why the Caged Bird Sings.* New York: Bantam, 1968. A moving coming-of-age novel about a young black girl in the American South.

Berrigan, Daniel. *No Bars to Manhood.* New York: Doubleday & Company, 1970. A priest's personal philosophy about the true meaning of courage.

Black, Claudia. *Children of Alcoholics: It Will Never Happen to Me.* New York: Balantine Books, 1981. Practical information about how to deal with alcoholism in your family.

Clark, Kenneth B. "An Interview with Martin Luther King, Jr." *King, Malcolm, Baldwin: Three Interviews* by Kenneth B. Clark, Wesleyan Press, 1963. Reprinted in *The Conscious Reader*, 4th edition, edited by Caroline Schroder, Harry Firestone and Michael Shugrue, New York: McMillan 1988, 716-723. Leading historian conducts a remarkable interview with Dr. Martin Luther King, Jr.

Gersoni-Stavin, Diane. *Sexism and Youth.* New York and London: R.R. Bowker Co., 1974. A collection of articles, including some written by high school students, about growing up in a sexist society.

Pinkham, Mary Ellen. *How to Stop the One You Love from Drinking*. New York: Berkley, 1989. Advice on how to help someone you love recover from alcoholism.

Student Press Law Center Report. Student Press Law Center, Suite 300, 800 18th Street NW, Washington, D.C., 20006, Spring 1988, Fall 1988, Winter 1988-89. Current information on your First Amendment Rights.

Williams, Juan. *Eyes on the Prize: America's Civil Rights Years, 1954-1965*. New York: Viking, 1987. Companion book to the popular documentary series on the history of the Civil Rights Movement.

INDEX

About the Author

Ellen Kahaner is a freelance writer living in New York City. Her
recent books include *What's So Bad About the Fourth Grade?* (Troll,
Inc.) and *Motorcycles* (Capstone Press).
She is currently working on a series of books about kids who are
actively trying to improve the quality of life in their communities.

Photo Credits and Acknowledgments
Cover photo: Blackbirch Graphics
Pages 2,6,9,15,17,19,20,22,28,31,32,36,38-39,42,53, Wide World; p.11,23,25,47,
S.FitzGerald; p.P.35, Bettman.

Design and Production: Blackbirch Graphics, Inc.